NORTH WEST RAILWAYS IN THE 1970s AND 1980s

JOHN CARLSON

AMBERLEY

On Sunday 27 December 1981 the last Deltic service across the Pennines is worked by No. 55009 (D9009) ALYCIDON. Seen here at Liverpool Lime Street.

First published 2021

Amberley Publishing
The Hill, Stroud
Gloucestershire, GL5 4EP

www.amberley-books.com

Copyright © John Carlson, 2021

The right of John Carlson to be identified as the Author of this work has been asserted in accordance with the Copyrights, Designs and Patents Act 1988.

ISBN 978 1 4456 8754 4 (print)
ISBN 978 1 4456 8755 1 (ebook)

British Library Cataloguing in Publication Data.
A catalogue record for this book is available from the British Library.

Origination by Amberley Publishing.
Printed in the UK.

Acknowledgements

Many people have helped with the putting together of this book. I would like to thank, in no order, Stuart Smith, Hugh McAuley, Charles Roberts and Martin Jenkins of the Online Transport Archive, and members of the Facebook group The North Rail Scene, who have helped with additional information and locations. I would also like to thank J. R. Carter and C. M. Whitehouse for their photographs. For various reasons this book has ventured slightly outside its original geographical remit; however, we think it is all the richer for that. Additional thanks go to Charles Loarridge and Craig Oliphant.

No. 25119 passing Chester No. 4 box on a ballast train, *c.* April 1984.

Introduction

This book has come out of my interest in transport photography. While I have travelled around the region taking my own photographs, except for one, none of those included here are mine. They are all otherwise images that have been bought, given or loaned to me by several groups and individuals over the years. The bulk of them were taken by Barrie Watkins, an excellent railway photographer who I have never met, but I bought quite a lot of his negatives from him via eBay several years ago. I remember him writing a brief note to me saying that I had bought some of his best work from him. He had travelled over much of the country shooting on black and white and occasionally colour film and although the reels were processed, he had never printed from them. He also added that he very much enjoyed scanning the preview images for eBay and seeing where he had been over the years.

After several years of looking at them and thinking 'I really must do something with these', I finally did, and this book began to take form. The images are focussed around the north-west of England but I have strayed out of that area a little to include some of Barrie's excellent images that would otherwise remain unseen. Although this books timeframe is around the 1970s and 1980s, I have also ventured slightly beyond British Rail.

A Class 31 locomotive and unknown crew members lay over at Manchester Victoria station. Victoria has been the subject of considerable change across the decades. It opened opened on 1 January 1844 and was named Victoria in 1843. By 1904 it had seventeen platforms. The current station front was built in 1909.

Manchester Victoria west signal box on 27 September 1981. Class 25 locomotive No. 25186 is seen. The view is towards the former Manchester Exchange station.

Class 25 locomotive No. 25097 at Manchester Victoria on 29 May 1979.

Manchester Victoria on 4 August 1977. The station's platform capacity was reduced by British Rail in the early 1970s, with platforms 1–3 being taken out of use and rail services started being transferring away from Victoria.

Class 47 locomotive No. 47052 on tanks runs through Manchester Victoria on 21 April 1979.

Class 25 No. 25032 on a line of empties with a crew change underway at Manchester Victoria on 27 September 1981.

Class 40 locomotive No. 40088 running through Manchester Victoria on 21 April 1976. The view is looking towards Manchester Exchange.

Class 31 locomotive No. 31275 at Manchester Victoria. The station suffered damaged by aerial bombardment during the Second World War. The roof and other areas were also damaged by the 1996 IRA bombing.

A Class 31 locomotive in Railfreight colours at Manchester Victoria. Date unknown. In 1992 construction of Manchester Arena began here, sweeping away almost every visible feature.

Class 25 locomotive No. 25097 sits at Manchester Victoria.

Class 31 locomotives Nos 31125 and 31164 at Manchester Victoria. Date unknown.

Class 25 locomotive No. 25249 at Manchester Victoria on 8 November 1975.

Class 47 No. 47303 on an excursion train at Manchester Victoria with a crew change taking place. The date is 27 September 1981.

Above: Locomotive No. 4472, more commonly known as the *Flying Scotsman*, at Manchester Victoria on 23 September 1973, with the bell fitted for its American tour still in place.

Left: Class 08 shunter No. 08676 at Manchester Victoria on 8 May 1982.

A Class 40 locomotive rests just outside Manchester Victoria station looking up Miles Platting. Manchester Victoria East Junction signal box is behind the loco. Date unknown.

Class 40 locomotive No. 40011 at Manchester Victoria on 25 July 1978.

Class 25 locomotive No. 25208 with an eastbound freight at Manchester Victoria on 29 May 1979.

An undated view of Manchester Victoria. This area has been radically transformed with the construction of Manchester Arena on this site from 1992. Platforms from the left of this image have been relocated into the centre of this area and it is now enclosed under the arena itself.

Class 304 EMU No. 041 on a Preston to Crewe service at Wigan on 30 August 1983.

Above: Empty TransPennine rolling stock arrives at Manchester Victoria on 21 October 1974.

Left: Class 40 locomotives Nos 40133 and 40137 at Carlisle on 24 March 1979.

Etterby, Carlisle, on 24 March 1979. High-speed train No. 254026 on an Up express, diverted due to the Penmanshiel Tunnel collapse.

The 13.45 Manchester Victoria to Bangor train at Winwick Junction on 19 April 1980.

The 14.13 Chester to Manchester Victoria at Winwick Junction on 19 April 1980.

Class 40 locomotive No. 40181 at Winwick Junction with two brake vans on 19 April 1980.

Class 87 locomotive No. 87021 at Winwick Junction with the Up Royal Scott at 10.10 on 19 April 1980.

Crew and Class 81 No. 81011 on 1 August 1977.

Above: Nos 83006 and 86024 double-head at Winwick Junction on tank waggons on 30 December 1979.

Right: Class 87 No. 87017 on a Down express at Etterby, Carlisle, on 23 April 1979.

Above: Class 87 locomotive No. 87027 at Acton Grange Junction on 30 August 1978.

Left: Class 89 locomotive No. 87032 awaits departure from Wigan on 30 August 1983.

Class 40 locomotive No. 40188 at Winwick Junction on 19 April 1980.

Class 08 shunter No. 08624 passes Winwick on 28 May 1977.

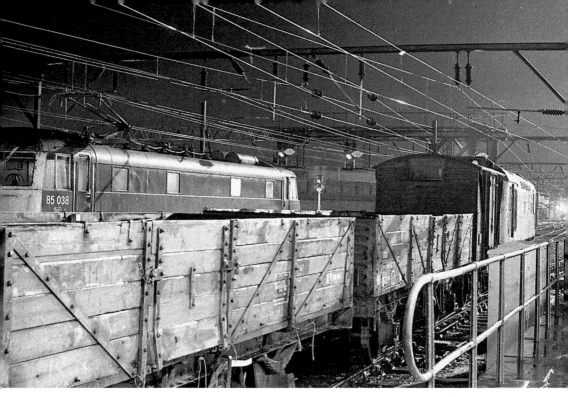

Locomotive No. 85038 with an Up-bound ICI train and No. 25093 with an Up-bound freight at Crewe on 28 December 1978.

Class 45 locomotive No. 45015 backs onto the 17.10 Liverpool Lime Street to Newcastle train on 20 March 1975.

Class 25 locomotives Nos 25110 and 25139 on a permanent way train pass through Olive Mount Cutting, Liverpool. The date is 7 September 1977.

A TransPennine express unit waits at Liverpool Lime Street. Date unknown.

A British Railways Blue Pullman unit waits to pull away at Liverpool Lime Street. Date unknown.

Warehouses, cranes and a Class 03 shunter. A riverside scene at Birkenhead.

Class 40 locomotive No. 40155 at Wigan with ICI tankers on 4 July 1979.

Class 25 locomotives Nos 25097 and 25112 with an Up cement train at Winwick Junction on 30 March 1978.

Above and below: British Railways electric locomotives Nos 27032 and 84010 seen here at Carlisle *c*. April 1980.

An undated view of Blacon station. Blacon station opened on 31 March 1890. It was closed to passengers by British Railways on 9 September 1968. Freight continued to use the line until 20 April 1984, then resumed on 31 August 1986. The railway closed completely in 1992 and is now a cycle path.

Class 40 locomotive No. 40163 on limestone traffic at Chinley on 18 April 1979. Damaged unit M51942 is under the tarpaulin to the right. It is believed the DMU had been irregularly hand-signalled past a red signal and then collided with a stationary freight train.

Above: Locomotives Nos 31156 and 81166 double-head Tilcon hoppers at Skipton on 2 August 1979.

Right: Southbound Class 25 locomotive No. 25184 with coal empties at Wigan on 8 June 1979.

Class 08 No. 08524 at Lostock on 14 April 1981.

Locomotive Nos 40028 and 40086 hauling the Border City Railtour stop at Garsdale for a photo opportunity on 24 March 1984. The tour was formed of No. 028+40086 Garsdale 1Z36 07.40 London Paddington to Carlisle, which was formed of twelve coaches & named 'The Border City' railtour by operator Class 50 Railtours.

Class 08 No. 08871 on empties passes Chesterfield on 27 August 1981.

Locomotives Nos 40095 and 47529 at Warrington Arpley Junction on 24 February 1976.

Locomotive No. 25044 hauling a northbound ballast train at Greenholme in 1984.

At Irlam yard on 2 June 1976, locomotive No. 47182 is at the head of a line of steel bogies for the steelworks.

No. 40188 at Wigan on a freight working. The date is 4 July 1979.

Locomotive No. 40035 Warcop headshunt on 9 June 1984.

A rather frozen break van passes through Warrington Bank Quay station on 5 January 1979.

Class 56 locomotive No. 56110 at Colling Green.

A Class 31 locomotive at Shrewsbury. Date unknown.

Class 25 locomotive No. 25296 taking coals into Agecroft Power Station on 24 June 1977.

Class 43 high-speed unit Nos 43039 (left) and 43093 (right) at Derby Works open day on 1 September 1979.

Nos 43124 and 86008 at Crewe Works on 7 December 1980.

High-speed trains under construction at Crewe Works on 7 December 1980.

Nos 25200 and 43133 at Derby Works on 24 January 1981.

Class 25 locomotive No. 25100 and Class 08 No. 08687 at Longsight Motive Power Depot on 8 June 1979.

A locomotive line up including Nos 40163, 40133 and 47045 at Crewe Works open day on 24 September 1977.

Blackpool North station on 14 June 1975. The 07.35 from York has just arrived.

Class 50 locomotive No. 50017 at Blackpool North on the 10.45 to Euston on 15 June 1975.

Opposite page: No. 50742 Leeds to Crewe train at Derby on 1 September 1979.

Above: Nos 56340 and 51190 at Helsby Junction on 24 August 1982.

The 15.33 Buxton to Manchester Piccadilly train at Heaton Chapel.

Bolton station's main building was demolished in the 1980s. The Victorian buildings are still standing. As of 2020 massive investment including overhead electrification has taken place.

A Blackpool-bound DMU at Bolton on 20 September 1981.

The 4.10 Liverpool to York service departing St Helen's Junction on 30 October 1975.

The 11.10 Liverpool to Hull service pauses at Selby on 20 March 1978.

Locomotive No. 45109 at South Dent signal box WA, Easter 1984.

New Mills Junction on 9 June 1976.

Class 25 No. 25109 on a goods train at Kirkham on 14 June 1975.

The 10.13 to Manchester Piccadilly at New Mills on 27 August 1982.

Class 86 locomotive No. 86255 pauses at Preston on an express working. The date is 5 December 1983.

Electric locomotives Nos 86314 and 87003 at Preston on 3 November 1982.

Preston station.

Class 50 locomotives Nos 50010 and 50045 at Preston on 13 June 1975.

No. 253021 passes through Reading on 31 May 1979.

High-speed locomotives Nos 253018 and 43037 at Reading on the Paddington to Weston-super-Mare train at 13.45 on 31 May 1979.

Above and below: Locomotive D200 No. 40122 working the Hardian Railtour, its first working since it was overhauled and repainted into the green livery that it carried throughout the rest of its career. Here it is running around its train at Warcop station on 31 July 1983. The presence of a police officer to accompany any train down the Warcop branch seemed to have been universal.

Class 56 locomotive No. 56092 on westbound coals for Gaston Dock at Guide Bridge. The date is 10 August 1983.

Class 08 shunting locomotive No. 08284 at Winwick Junction on 18 February 1980.

Class 40 locomotive No. 40181 with a container train at Winwick Junction on 18 February 1980.

Class 46 locomotive No. 46031 at Derby with the 10.55 Weymouth to Leeds service on 1 September 1979.

Above: Class 08 locomotive No. 08330 at Toton on 24 January 1981.

Left: Class 47 No. 47374 at Chesterfield on 27 August 1981.

On 28 December 1978 a Preston Barrow train calls in at Arnside on 28 December 1978.

On 21 June 1980 a DMU to Liverpool passes through Patricroft station. This part of the Liverpool & Manchester Railway was later electrified in stages between 2013 and 2015.

Above: A British Railways 101 DMU resplendent in BR blue at platform 11, Chester station.

Left: A DMU service for Rock Ferry station at Helsby on 24 August 1982. The station has won numerous Best Kept Station awards and is a Grade II listed building.

Manchester Victoria station prior to the closure of the side-contact electric rail system to Bury in 1991. After closure the line was converted into part of the Manchester Metrolink system, which has since continued to expand and renew itself for several decades.

A Metrolink T68 tram and a Class 158 DMU quite possibly on a TransPennine service at Manchester Victoria. Although 'money had been spent' on the station, there was still an overall feeling of dereliction and neglect about the place, which took a modernisation program over two decades later to dispel.

Bowker Vale station. It opened on 26 September 1938 to serve the growing number of local to houses, and closed on 17 August 1991 with the conversion of the line to Metrolink.

Heaton Park station in the latter days of the side-contact rail electric system. The electric system was installed in response to competition from local electric trams. This station is now part of the Manchester Metrolink system.

Construction underway on Manchester Metrolink's Queens Road depot. The depot lies next to the Bury line between Victoria and Woodlands Road. The date is likely to be around 1991.

Bury Interchange. The station opened in 1980 and also incorporates a bus interchange. It opened as part of the Metrolink network on 6 April 1992, with tram services later extending from Manchester Victoria across the city to Altringham.

A Metrolink Tram runs into Bury Interchange. The bridge above the tram carries the heritage East Lancashire Railway.

This page and overleaf: The images on these two pages show the rebuilding of Manchester Victoria station around 1990 to allow it to become part of the Metrolink network. Platforms 5 to 8 were reconstructed to take the Metrolink service. The trams then ran into the city via a sharp curve and a newly constructed gap in the station wall. In 2009 the station was later named as one of the worst regional interchanges in the UK. It has since been drastically rebuilt with a new overall roof and enlarged tram stop.

Metrolink construction underway in the Shudehill area. The Metrolink line became operational in 1992 but it was over ten years before a tram stop opened here on 31 March 2003. The bus interchange opened on 29 January 2006.

A Metrolink tram is pulled passed The Grand Hotel on Aytoun Street by the system's SPV. This is likely to be a gauging test before the overhead power was fully turned on to test the trams could run on the route without hitting obstacles.

Test runs on Metrolink between Pomona tram stop and Cornbrook Metrolink station.

The G-Mex tram stop around 1997. The Metrolink system has helped make Manchester a place that appeals to people from all around the world.

Class 86 locomotive No. 86211 passes No. 86252 on a Glasgow-bound service at Warrington on 3 January 1979.

Class 87 locomotive No. 87006 on the 09.15 Euston to Glasgow train passes Winwick Junction on 18 February 1980.

A Class 87 locomotive at Crewe South.

At Acton Grange Junction on 30 August 1978 Class 87 No. 87027 is on the 10.45 Glasgow to Euston.

The National Tramway Museum, Crich. The personnel are (from left to right): Merlyn Bacon, President Chaceley Humpidge , George Hearse, Major Charles Walker and Basil Miller. This is likely to be a posed photograph against the newly repainted Blackpool 49.

Former Blackpool TV car 17 at Crich. It has since been restored as Blackpool toast rack car 166.

A line up of tramcars and works vehicles at Crich in the museum's earlier days.

Blackpool Standard No. 40 in the snow.

Locomotive No. 4472, more commonly known as the *Flying Scotsman*, departing from Chester.

Locomotive No. 4472 at Guide Bridge Yard getting ready to run to York.

No. 4472 departs from Victoria station.

The view from the cab as a Hull to Manchester train passes through Hope station on 18 April 1979.

Diesel and electric units at Davenport station in this undated view.

Above: Class 24 locomotive No. 24020 on a westbound goods service at Manchester Victoria. The date is 21 October 1974.

Right: Class 40 locomotive No. 40031 approaching Manchester Victoria on a westbound goods service. The date is 21 October 1974.

Class 24 locomotive No. 24020 on a westbound goods service approaches Manchester Victoria. The date is 24 October 1974.

A double-headed freight runs past Woodhead signal box on the Woodhead line.

Class 76 locomotives Nos 76055, 76041 and 76040 at Reddish Electric Depot on 29 October 1978.

Torside on the Woodhead line. The date is 2 June 1976.

A Class 50 locomotive runs into Preston station.

Preston station.

Preston station.

Class 87 locomotive No. 87010 at Crewe on the 17.55 Euston to Manchester service on 28 December 1978.

Manchester Victoria on 27 September 1981. Locomotive No. 40155 approaches with a goods train.

Class 47 locomotive No. 47290 and Class 08 shunter No. 08475 at Manchester Victoria on 21 October 1974.

Class 50 locomotive No. 50040 and Class 86 electric locomotive No. 86027 on a Euston to Inverness diversion passing through Manchester Victoria at 09.35 on 9 August 1975.

Class 47 locomotive No. 47083 and Class 87 No. 87203 at Manchester Victoria with a diverted train on 27 August 1981.

A disused Manchester Central station in 1978.

A Class 31 locomotive at Manchester Piccadilly station. Date unknown.

Blackpool works car No. 5 at Rigby Road depot. It was built as a passenger car in 1934. In 1965 it became permanent way car No. 5, then was rebuilt as a one-man-operated car in 1972. It is now in storage at Crich.

Hill of Howth No. 10 at Blackpool in 1984. It was regauged to 4 feet 8.5 inches prior to its visit. The car is now on static display at Crich.

1937 Blackpool Brush car No. 633 on the Promenade at North Pier, c. 1984. The car is wearing one of a number of distinctive all-over advertising liveries carried by it and other cars at Blackpool.

Manchester Corporation Tramways No. 765 at the central pier. It was built to cope with routes in Manchester with low bridges. The body is largely original, although the truck is a regauged Hill of Howth original. It is normally at the Heaton Park Tramway, but has also run at Beamish and Blackpool.

Locomotive No. 40152 hauling a failed Diesel Multiple Unit at Chester.

A tanker train at Shap in 1971. (Photograph by Les Folkard)

Class 25 locomotive No. 25188 at Horwich Works on 16 August 1980.

A Manchester to Southport train arrives at Wigan on 8 June 1977.

Class 40 locomotive No. 40018 departing Eccles station at 15.40 on a Manchester to Bangor train on 3 April 1980.

Oxford Road station on 13 June 1975. The station was rebuilt in 1960, then again in the early 1970s after the closure of Manchester Central station. There are plans to rebuild the line as part of the Northern Hub.

No. 042 on the 2H53 Manchester Oxford Road to Alderley Edge train on 13 June 1975.

No. 042 on the 2H53 to Alderney Edge at Oxford Road on 13 June 1975.

No. 025 to Altringham at Manchester Oxford Road on 13 June 1975.

Departing Birmingham for Manchester via Stoke on 10 June 1976.

Locomotive No. 25189 with loaded waggons at Ribblehead Quarry, *c.* 1983.

Class 40 locomotive No. 40096 crossing the River Kent on Arnside Viaduct. The date is 29 August 1978. Constructed in 1856 as a single-line viaduct, the structure was extended to twin track in 1863. In more recent years the viaduct has been the site of unofficial Christmas and Boxing Day walks.

A Class 25 locomotive No. 25205 hauls a Mk 2 coach at Preston on 25 August 1982.

Class 25 locomotives Nos 25151 and 25149 at Wigan with an Up cement train on 8 June 1977.

Class 47 locomotive No. 47527 at Eccles with a Liverpool to Newcastle train on 17 April 1980.

Class 45 locomotive No. 45119 departs from Leicester for St Pancras on 29 October 1981.

Bidston station has closed twice during its existence, due to low passenger numbers. It opened on 2 July 1866 as a terminus, then closed on 4 July 1870. It reopened on 1 August 1872. It closed again in June 1890 and reopened again on 18 May 1896. In 1898 Bidston became a through station when the line was extended to Seacombe and became a passenger interchange.